W9-CHJ-898

France

TERESA FISHER

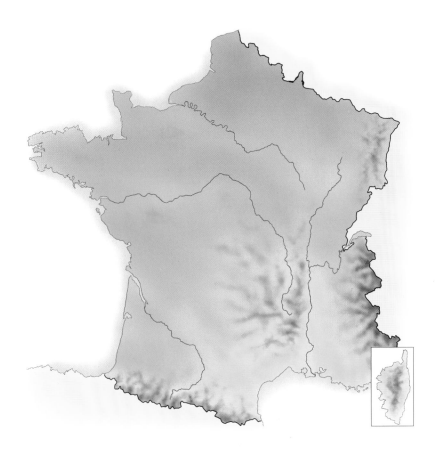

RSVP
RAINTREE
STECK-VAUGHN
P U B L I S H E R S
A Steck-Vaughn Company

Austin, Texas

WE COME FROM

Brazil • China • France
Germany • India • Jamaica • Japan
Kenya • Nigeria • South Africa

Most of the people you are about to meet live in a city in France called Toulouse. Like any other country, France has many different types of lifestyles. People live in the country as well as in towns and cities.

Cover: Pierre and his friends have some fun on their bicycles at the side of the Garonne River.

Title page (from top to bottom): Shoppers search for bargains at the flea market in Toulouse; wild goats graze in the Pyrénées; people relax outside a café in Aix-en-Provence; a master chocolate maker shows his chocolate clowns; and a woman buys some fish from an indoor food market.

Contents page: A woman looks for shellfish on the beach.

Index: The Batiste family sets off on a bicycle ride.

Published by Raintree Steck-Vaughn Publishers, an imprint of Steck-Vaughn Company

Printed in Italy. Bound in the United States.
1 2 3 4 5 6 7 8 9 0 04 03 02 01 00

Library of Congress Cataloging-in-Publication Data
Fisher, Teresa
France / Teresa Fisher.
    p.   cm.—(We come from)
    Includes bibliographical references and index.
    Summary: Introduces the land, climate, industries, home life, schools, and recreations of France.
    ISBN 0-8172-5212-6
    1. France—Civilization—Juvenile literature.
    [1. France.]
    I. Title. II. Series.
    DC33.7.F5   1999
    944—dc21   98-46690

Picture Acknowledgments: All the photographs in this book were taken by Dorian Shaw. The map artwork on page 5 was produced by Peter Bull.

Contents

Introduction

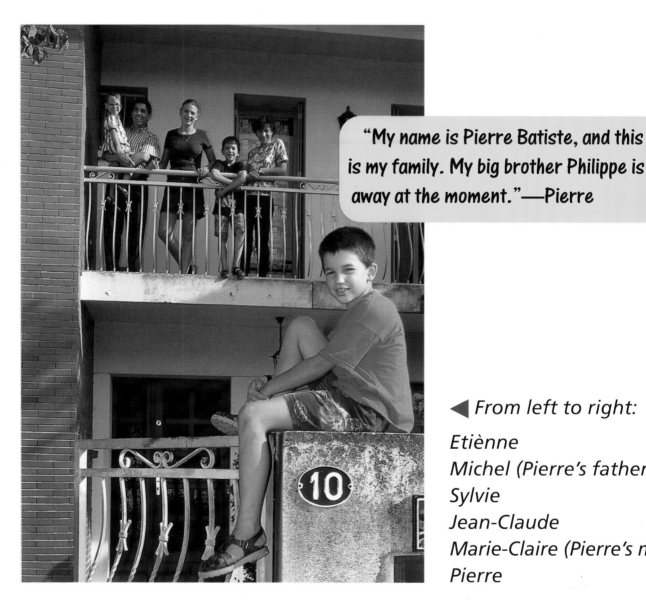

"My name is Pierre Batiste, and this is my family. My big brother Philippe is away at the moment."—Pierre

◀ *From left to right:*

Etiènne
Michel (Pierre's father)
Sylvie
Jean-Claude
Marie-Claire (Pierre's mom)
Pierre

Pierre is nine years old. He lives near Toulouse with his parents, his three brothers, Etiènne, Jean-Claude, and Philippe, and his sister, Sylvie. Toulouse is a large city in southern France. You can see where it is on the map on page 5.

▶ *France's place in the world*

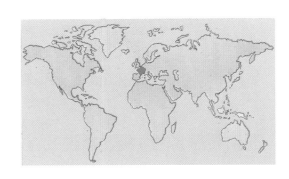

▼ *This book takes you to Toulouse as well as the rest of France.*

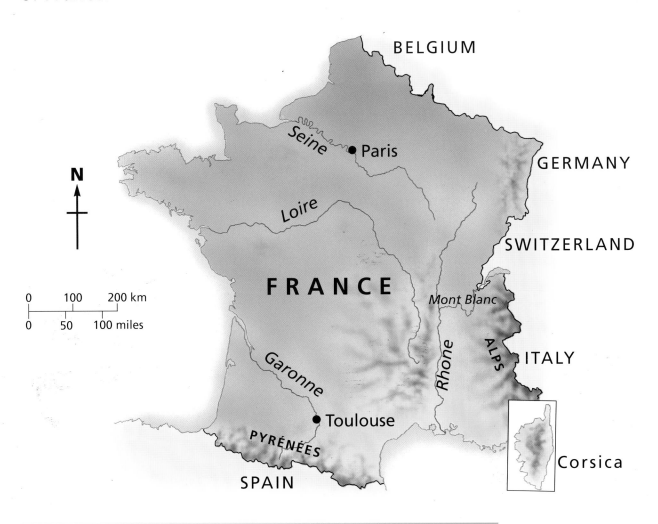

FRANCE

Capital city:	Paris
Land area:	212,918 sq. mi. (551,458 sq. km)
Population:	58 million people
Main language:	French
Main religion:	Roman Catholicism

The Land and Weather

France is the largest country in Western Europe. It is bordered by Spain, Germany, Switzerland, Luxembourg, and Belgium.

Most large cities in France are near its coast or along a river.

▼ *Many French people spend their vacations in France.*

▲ *Toulouse lies on the Garonne River.*

In the south of France, the summers are long, warm, and dry, and the winters are mild and rainy. The weather is cooler and wetter in the north.

▲ *During the winter, snow covers the Pyrénées Mountains.*

▲ *There are many pig farms near Toulouse.*

France has more farmland than any other country in Europe. The main crops are wheat, barley, grapes, and apples. Dairy farmers make many different kinds of cheeses. Pig farmers produce lots of different types of sausages.

"I use this tool to check that my goat cheese is ready to eat."
—Jean-Luc, cheesemaker

Around Toulouse, where Pierre lives, there are hills, woodland, and meadows. To the south are the high mountains of the Pyrénées. To the southeast, there are the sandy beaches of the Mediterranean.

▼ *French apples are sold all over the world.*

Home Life

Most people in France live in large towns and cities where the homes are mainly apartments. They don't usually have yards, but often have balconies where the family can sit or hang the laundry.

In the suburbs, just outside the cities, some people live in houses or bungalows.

▲ Many people in France live in apartments like these.

◀ In villages, some people live in old stone cottages and farmhouses.

▶ This woman has planted lots of flowers on her balcony.

Pierre's family lives in a house in the suburbs of Toulouse. It has a large living room, kitchen, bathroom, four bedrooms, and a sunny balcony. Pierre shares a bedroom with his brother Philippe.

"Sharing a room is fine. My brother is usually out, so I can have friends to visit."
—Pierre

◄ Pierre often helps his mother around the house.

Pierre's family spends a lot of time together. On weekends, they often visit friends or go bicycling in the countryside.

In the evenings, the children often stay up late, reading, watching television, or talking with their parents at the dinner table.

◄ Pierre's mother does her sewing in peace and quiet.

Food and Cooking

French people love their food and wine. France is well known for its delicious cooking, using fresh food from colorful local markets.

▶ *French people often like to relax in outside cafés and restaurants.*

"My customers know that everything on my vegetable stand is fresh. That's why they keep coming back!"—Mr. Dupont, grocer

◀ *Delicious hot pancakes, called* crêpes, *are a favorite snack.*

One typical French dish is snails, served hot with garlic butter. *Crêpes* and pâté are popular foods. France is famous for mushrooms called truffles. Pigs are used to sniff them out. Truffles are expensive and are eaten only on special occasions.

The Batiste family always starts the day with breakfast. Usually they have a long, thin, crusty loaf of fresh bread called a baguette, with a bowl of coffee or hot chocolate.

▲ Chocolate éclairs *are filled with delicious cream.*

"For a treat we have croissants for breakfast on weekends."
—Pierre

The main meal is usually dinner in the evening, when the whole family gets together. But on Sundays, they have a huge midday lunch with four to five courses. This meal sometimes lasts all afternoon.

▲ *Pierre and his family sit down to eat lunch together.*

Working Hard

France is well known for making airplanes, cars, and trains. But it is even more famous for making goods, such as perfume, cheeses, wine, and champagne. These goods are sold all over the world.

▲ *A customer carefully chooses some perfume.*

▼ *There is a huge selection of cheeses in France.*

Most people in Toulouse work in the banks, stores, or companies in the downtown area. Many people work in big factories outside the city.

Pierre's father works for an insurance company. He spends four days each week traveling to see customers and one day working at home.

School

Classes usually start at half-past-eight in the morning and end at half-past-four in the afternoon.

Most schools have a two-hour lunchbreak. Some children go home for lunch, while others have their lunch at school.

▼ *There's always a wait to use the school computers.*

▲ *Pierre walks to school with his mother and friends.*

Pierre goes to elementary school near his home. It is a large school with more than 500 pupils. There are about 30 boys and girls in Pierre's class. Pierre's favorite class is computer studies.

▼ *This is Pierre's geography class.*

The children sometimes spend their spare time in the school library.

On Wednesday afternoons, children can play sports or take part in activities such as painting, drama, or dance at local youth clubs. Most schools have classes on Saturday mornings.

These children are learning karate at a youth club.

"I normally do about an hour's homework every night before dinner."—Pierre

Spare Time

The French love sports, especially soccer and bicycling. Most French families spend their vacations in France, in the mountains, or at the beach.

In his spare time, Pierre has fun with his friends, watching television, going to the movies, reading comics, and playing lots of sports.

▲ *Surfing is a popular weekend sport.*

▶ *In-line skating is the latest craze in France.*

"I love playing computer games. My friend, Lucas, is always trying to beat my score."
—Pierre

24

Looking Ahead

"I love cycling. One day I want to ride in a bike race like the Tour de France."
—Pierre

France will always be famous for its food, fashion, industry, and farming.

Now more and more visitors are coming to France, to see some of its attractions, such as its beaches, ski resorts, and EuroDisney.

▶ The modern Cité de l'Espace (Space City) theme park in Toulouse is popular.

27

How to Play *Boules*

Boules is the national game of France. It can be played outside on any area of flat ground, with small groups of friends. These are the rules:

- Everyone stands behind a line.

- The first player throws a small wooden ball called a *cochonnet*, or "piglet," a short distance.

- He then throws the first *boule* (ball) as close to the piglet as possible.

▶ *Pierre's dad explains the rules.*

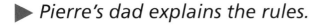

- The second player tries to throw the boule even closer to the piglet.

- All the other players take turns throwing their boules. Sometimes they aim to knock the other player's boules away from the piglet.

- The winner is the person whose boule is closest to the piglet at the end.

◀ *Pierre tries to throw his boule as close as possible to the piglet.*

France Fact File

Money Facts

France's money is the Franc, which is divided into 100 centimes. One dollar is about the same as 6 francs. If you look closely at a 50-franc note, you will see a tiny picture of the Little Prince, from the famous book of the same name, as well as the French author, Antoine de Saint-Exupéry.

Famous People

Famous French people include Napoléon (an army general who became emperor) and Charles Perrault who wrote *Sleeping Beauty* and *Cinderella*. Perhaps you have heard of them.

Stamps

▲ Most French stamps are red or blue with a picture of "Marianne" on them. Marianne is not a real person. She is a symbol of the French Republic. Some stamps have pretty pictures or cartoons on them.

◀ The French Flag

The French flag or *Tri-colore* ("three-colored") is red, white, and blue. Red and blue represent the city of Paris and white was the traditional color for the French kings of old.

Mountain Facts

The highest mountain in France is Mont Blanc, in the Alps —15,771 ft. (4,807 m).

River Facts

The longest rivers are the Loire, the Rhône, the Seine, and the Garonne.

The Seine is 482 mi. (776 km) long. ▶

The Fastest Trains in the World

French trains (called TGVs) are the fastest in the world, reaching speeds of up to 186 mph (300 km/h).

Bastille Day

There are more than 400 festivals in France. The biggest one is Bastille Day, on July 14. This festival celebrates France's becoming a Republic. A republic is governed by a chosen president, not ruled by a king or queen.

Cheese Selection

◀ There are more than 365 cheeses in France— a different one for every day of the year!

29

Glossary

Balcony A platform outside a window, usually with railings.

Border The imaginary line dividing two countries.

Bungalow A house on one floor.

Flea market A street market where people can buy second-hand goods.

Latest craze The most popular thing at the moment.

Pâté A paste made from mashed and spiced meat.

Suburbs Areas of houses and shops at the edge of a town or city.

Tour de France A special bicycle race across France that takes place every year.

Traditional Having been done in a certain way for a very long time.

Further Information

Boast, Clare. *France* (Next Stop). New York: Heinemann Library, 1998.

Bussolin, Veronique. *France* (Country Fact Files). Austin, TX: Raintree Steck-Vaughn, 1995.

Denny, Roz. *A Taste of France* (Food Around the World). Austin, TX: Raintree Steck-Vaughn, 1997.

Fisher, Teresa. *France* (Country Insights). Austin, TX: Raintree Steck-Vaughn, 1997.

Ganeri, Anita. *France* (Country Topics for Craft Projects). Danbury, CT: Franklin Watts, 1995.

Haskins, James. *Count Your Way Through France*. Minneapolis, MN: Carolrhoda Books, 1996.

Powell, Jillian. *A History of France Through Art*. Austin, TX: Thomson Learning, 1995.

Fiction
Dickens, Charles. *A Tale of Two Cities*

Dumas, Alexander. *The Three Musketeers*

Perrault, Charles. *Cinderella*

Useful Addresses
French Embassy and Consulate
4101 Reservoir Road
Washington, DC 20007
202-944-6000

French Government Tourist Office
610 Fifth Avenue
New York, NY 10020
212-838-7800

Index

All the numbers in **bold** refer to photographs.